W9-CQF-732

Nita Mehta's

Indian
COOKING

Nita Mehta

B.Sc. (Home Science), M.Sc. (Food and Nutrition), Gold Medalist

Tanya Mehta

SNAB
Publishers Pvt Ltd

Nita Mehta's
Indian
cooking

©Copyright 2003-2004 **SNAB** Publishers Pvt Ltd

WORLD RIGHTS RESERVED. The contents—all recipes, photographs and drawings are original and copyrighted. No portion of this book shall be reproduced, stored in a retrieval system or transmitted by any means, electronic, mechanical, photocopying, recording or otherwise, without the written permission of the publishers.

While every precaution is taken in the preparation of this book, the publisher and the author assume no responsibility for errors or omissions. Neither is any liability assumed for damages resulting from the use of information contained herein.

TRADEMARKS ACKNOWLEDGED. Trademarks used, if any, are acknowledged as trademarks of their respective owners. These are used as reference only and no trademark infringement is intended upon.

Reprint 2004
ISBN 81-7869-046-2

Food Styling and Photography: **SNAB**

Layout and laser typesetting :

National Information Technology Academy
3A/3, Asaf Ali Road
New Delhi-110002
☎ 23252948

Distributed by :

THE VARIETY BOOK DEPOT
A.V.G. Bhavan, M 3 Con Circus,
New Delhi - 110 001
Tel : 23417175, 23412567; Fax : 23415335
Email: varietybookdepot@rediffmail.com

Published by :

Publishers Pvt. Ltd.
3A/3 Asaf Ali Road,
New Delhi - 110002
Tel: 23252948, 23250091
Telefax:91-11-23250091

Editorial and Marketing office:
E-159, Greater Kailash-II, N.Delhi-48
Fax: 91-11-29225218, 29229558
Tel: 91-11-29214011, 29218727, 29218574
E-Mail: nitamehta@email.com
snab@snabindia.com
Website: http://www.nitamehta.com
Website: http://www.snabindia.com

Printed by :

INTERNATIONAL PRINT-O-PAC LTD.

Rs. 89/-

Introduction

*I*ndian cuisine is a favourite not only in India but its popularity is also spreading to all parts of the globe. The Tandoori Murg and Curry culture is fast spreading all over the world. People in London and New York are getting acquainted with Indian food.

The book contains delicacies which, though exotic, are easy to prepare. I have used exotic Indian spices to create dishes with a special flavour and aroma. All the recipes have been created using the simplest ingredients and techniques. The recipes are simple and quick and yet extravagant and exotic.

Nita Mehta

ABOUT THE RECIPES

WHAT'S IN A CUP?

INDIAN CUP
1 teacup = 200 ml liquid
AMERICAN CUP
1 cup = 240 ml liquid (8 oz.)
The recipes in this book were tested with the Indian teacup which holds 200 ml liquid.

Contents

Vegetables 24

Chicken, Mutton & Fish 51

Snacks 77

VEGETARIAN

Special Paneer Pakore 78
Dahi Bade 82
Soya Balls 87

NON VEGETARIAN

Besani Murgi 80
Chicken Lollipops 84

Roti & Biryani 88

VEGETARIAN

Lachha Parantha 89
Nan Badaami 90
Tandoori Platter with
BBQ Sauce 96

NON VEGETARIAN

Khasta Keema Parantha 92
Chicken Kali Mirch Pulao 94

Sweets 99

Jalebi with Rabri 100

Phirni 102

Tandoori

Tips for perfect tandoori cooking ....

- Tandoori food should be barbecued on the grill rack or wire rack (*jaali*) of the oven and not on the oven tray. Food does not get crisp when put onn a tray. When it is on the wire rack, the liquid drips down, making it crisp. These drippings can be collected on a tray covered with aluminium foil and placed under the rack.

- Cut pieces of food according to the space in between wires of the grill. If the distance between the wires of rack is too wide, then your piece can slip. So cover the wire rack with a well greased **aluminium foil**.

- The size of tikkas should not be **too small**. After getting cooked they shrink. A very small piece after getting cooked can turn hard.

- While skewering or placing pieces of vegetables, the pieces should be arranged such that there is atleast **1" gap** between them so that each piece can get it's own space and heat all around to get cooked properly.

- When skewering vegetables, it is advisable to use **thinner skewers**, then there is less chance of chicken, fish or vegetable to break.

Akbari Kebabs: Recipe on page 14 ➤

Achaari Paneer Tikka

Pickled flavoured masala paneer tikka.

Makes 10-12

400 gms paneer - cut into 1½" rectangles of ¾-1" thickness

ACHAARI MASALA

1 tbsp saunf (aniseeds), ½ tsp sarson (mustard seeds)
a pinch of methi daana (fenugreek seeds)
½ tsp kalonji (onion seeds), ½ tsp jeera (cumin seeds)

OTHER INGREDIENTS

1 cup curd - hang in a muslin cloth for ½ hour
1 onion - chopped finely
2 green chillies - chopped
2 tsp ginger-garlic paste
1 tsp cornflour
½ tsp haldi (turmeric) powder, 1 tsp amchoor (dried mango powder)
1 tsp dhania powder, ½ tsp garam masala

Contd...

1 tsp salt or to taste, ½ tsp sugar
some chaat masala to sprinkle
some melted butter/oil for basting the tikkas

1. Collect all the seeds of achaari masala together.
2. Heat 2 tbsp oil. Add the collected seeds together to the hot oil. Let saunf change colour.
3. Add onions & green chillies. Cook till onions turn golden brown.
4. Reduce heat. Add haldi, amchoor, dhania powder, garam masala, salt and sugar. Mix. Remove from fire. Let it cool down.
5. Beat curd till smooth. Add garlic-ginger paste and cornflour. Add the onion masala also to the curd.
6. Add the paneer cubes to the curd. Marinate till serving time.
7. At serving time, rub oil generously over the grill of the oven or wire rack of a gas tandoor. Place paneer on greased wire rack or grill of the oven.
8. Heat an oven to 180°C or a gas tandoor on moderate flame. Grill paneer for 15 minutes. Spoon some oil or melted butter on the paneer pieces in the oven or tandoor and grill further for 5 minutes. Serve hot sprinkled with chaat masala.

Akbari Kebabs

Chicken breasts stuffed with a spiced cheese filling.

Picture on page 11   *Serves 4*

2 chicken breasts (300gm)

IST MARINADE
1 tbsp lemon juice, ½ tsp salt, ½ tsp red chilli powder

2ND MARINADE
1 cup thick curd - hung for 15-20 minutes
¼ cup thick cream, 2 tbsp grated cheese
1 tsp shah jeera (black cumin) - roughly crushed
1 tbsp cornflour
1 tsp red chilli powder, 1 tsp salt, a pinch of haldi, 1 tsp garam masala
1 tbsp ginger-garlic paste
1 tbsp barbecue masala or tandoori masala (optional)
2 tbsp coriander - chopped

FILLING
1 onion - cut into rings & then cut rings into half, 1 tbsp coriander - chopped

1 tsp shah jeera (black cumin), 100 gm cheese - finely grated
1 tsp ginger-garlic paste, 1 tbsp coriander

1. Open the breast slices to get thin big pieces (you can ask your butcher to do it for you). Cut each breast into 4 long strips, about 1½" wide, to make rolls.
2. Wash and pat dry the chicken strips.
3. Marinate the chicken with the all the ingredients of the first marinade
4. Mix the ingredients of the 2nd marinade together in a bowl.
5. Pick up the chicken pieces from the first marinade and squeeze gently. Put them in the curd-cream marinade in the bowl.
6. For the filling, heat 1½ tbsp oil. Add shah jeera. Let it change colour. Add onion. Cook till onion turns soft. Add ginger-garlic paste and coriander. Cook for 1 minute. Remove from fire. Add cheese.
7. To make the kebab, take a strip of chicken. Place 1 tbsp of filling on one end of the chicken strip & roll it forward tightly to form a roll. Place the roll on the greased wire rack. Pat the remaining marinade on the rolls.
8. Heat an oven to 180°C. Grill for ½ hour, turning and basting with melted butter or oil after 15-20 minutes. Cook till tender.

Subz Kakori

Very soft and delicious vegetarian seekh kebabs.

Serves 4-5

3 potatoes (medium) - boiled
(250 gm) 2 cups jimikand (yam) - chopped and boiled
½ cup crumbled paneer
4 tbsp cashewnuts (kaju) - ground
2 tsp ginger - garlic paste
1 big onion - very finely chopped (1 cup)
2 green chillies - very finely chopped
2 tbsp green coriander - very finely chopped
1 tsp bhuna jeera (cumin roasted)
1 tsp red chilli powder, ¼ tsp amchoor
2 bread slices - crumbled in a grinder to get fresh crumbs
1½ tsp salt, or to taste
a pinch of tandoori red colour

BASTING (POURING ON THE KEBABS)
1 - 2 tbsp melted butter or oil

1.   Boil the potatoes. Peel and mash.
2.   Pressure cook chopped yam with ½ cup water and ½ tsp salt to give 3 whistles. Remove from fire. After the pressure drops, keep it on fire to dry, if there is any excess water. Mash it to a paste.
3.   Mix mashed potatoes, yam and all other ingredients, making a slightly stiff dough.
4.   Oil and wipe the skewers. Heat the gas tandoor or oven. Remove the wire rack. Press into sausage-shaped kebabs on the skewers and cook for about 5 minutes in a hot oven at 180°C or a gas tandoor. Pour some melted butter on the kebabs to baste them when they get half done. Turn side and grill for 5-7 minutes or till golden brown. If you do not wish to grill the kebabs, shallow fry in 2 tbsp oil in a pan on low heat, turning sides till browned evenly.
5.   Sprinkle some tandoori or chaat masala and serve with onion rings and lemon wedges.

Note: Turn kebabs on the skewers only after they are half done, otherwise they tend to break.

Mutton Seekh

Succulent cocktail kebabs of lamb mince.

Picture on page 29   *Serves 4- 6*

½ kg lamb mince (keema)
2 onions - sliced, deep fried to a crisp brown colour and crushed
2 tsp ginger-garlic paste
2 tsp kaaju (cashewnuts) and 2 tsp khus khus(poppy seeds) - soak together for
15 minutes in a little warm water and grind to a fine paste
1 tsp garam masala powder or tandoori masala
1 tbsp kachri powder or 1 tbsp raw papaya paste (green papita) - peel, deseed
and grind a small piece of raw papaya in a mixer
2 tsp thick cream or mala,
salt to taste

DRY MASALA (MIX TOGETHER) TO SPRINKLE ON TOP
1 tsp salt, ½ tsp kala namak (rock salt)
½ tsp roasted jeera powder(bhuna jeera)
¼ tsp red chilli powder, ¼ tsp citric powder

BASTING (pouring on the kebabs) - 2 tbsp melted butter

1. Wash the mince in a strainer and gently press to squeeze out all the water. Grind in a grinder to make it fine.
2. Mix all ingredients- onions, ginger-garlic paste, kaju-khus khus paste, garam masala, papaya paste, cream and salt to the mince and knead well. Keep aside for 1 hour.
3. Heat the electric oven with greased skewers at 180°C.
4. Take a big ball of the mince mixture and hold a hot skewer carefully in the other hand. Press the mince on to the skewer. The mince will immediately stick to the skewer.
5. Make another seekh on the same skewer, leaving a gap of 2". Repeat with the left over mince on all the other skewers.
6. Place the skewers in the hot oven. Cook for 10-15 minutes, rotating the skewers and basting with melted butter in between. Cook for another 5 minutes. When cooked, gently remove the kebab from the skewers with the help of a cloth.
7. Shallow fry the seekh kebabs on non stick pan or tawa in 1-2 tbsp oil till golden brown.
8. Mix all masalas of the dry masala and keep aside. To serve kebabs, sprinkle some dry masala and lemon juice on the hot kebabs.

Special Shami Kebab (veg)

Serves 4

½ cup kale chane (black gram)
1 tbsp chane ki dal (bengal gram split)
1 onion - very finely chopped
1 tsp oil
1 tsp ginger paste, ½ tsp garlic paste
2 slices bread - grind in a mixer to get fresh crumbs
salt to taste
¼ tsp amchoor (dried mango powder)

GRIND TOGETHER TO A COARSE POWDER
¼ tsp jeera, 1" stick dalchini
3-4 laung (cloves)
3-4 saboot kali mirch (peppercorns), seeds of 2 moti illaichi
1 dry, red chilli

FILLING
2 tbsp finely chopped mint (poodina), 4 tbsp grated mozzarella cheese

1. Soak kale channe with channe ki dal overnight or for 6-8 hours in water.
2. Put kale channe, channe ki dal, onion and oil in a pressure cooker. Add powdered spices and 1½ cups water also. Pressure cook to give 1 whistle. After the first whistle, keep on slow fire for 20 minutes. Remove from fire and let the pressure drop by itself.
3. If there is extra water, dry the channas for sometime on fire. There should just be a little water, enough to grind the channas to a fine paste.
4. Grind to a fine paste.
5. Remove channa mixture to a bowl. Add ginger-garlic paste, bread, salt and amchoor to taste.
6. Mix all ingredients of the filling together.
7. Make a small ball of the paste. Flatten it, put 1 tsp of filling. Press the filling. Pick up the sides and make a ball again. Flatten it slightly.
8. Shallow fry 4-5 pieces on a tawa in 3-4 tbsp oil on medium flame.
9. Serve with poodina chutney.

Note: If the kebabs break on frying, roll in dry maida alone or in egg white first and then in maida. Fry on moderate heat.

Mahi (fish) Tikka

Serves 6-8

500 gm boneless singhara or sole fish - cut into 2" cubes
3 tbsp besan, 1 tbsp lemon juice

1ST MARINADE

2 tbsp vinegar or lemon juice
¼-½ tsp red chilli powder, ¼ tsp salt

2ND MARINADE

½ cup curd curd- hang in a muslin cloth for 15 minutes
¼ cup thick cream or malai
2 tsp ginger-garlic paste
½ tsp garam masala powder
½ tsp ajwain (carom seeds)
1 tsp salt, ½ tsp pepper
TO SPRINKLE, some chaat masala

1. Rub the fish well with 3 tbsp besan and 2 tbsp lemon juice to remove the fishy odour. Keep aside for 15 minutes. Wash well and pat dry on

a kitchen towel. Prick fish all over with a fork or give shallow cuts with a knife.

2. Sprinkle all the ingredients of the 1st marinade on the fish and mix. Keep aside for ½ hour.
3. In a bowl mix all the ingredients of the 2nd marinade.
4. Pick up the tikka pieces and add to the marinade in the bowl, mix to coat fish well with this marinade. Keep aside for 3-4 hours.
5. Heat an electric oven to 160°C or a gas tandoor on gas on low heat.
6. Skewer tikkas or place them on a well greased wire grill and roast till coating turns dry and golden brown. Baste with a little butter in between. Roast for another 2-3 minutes. Serve hot sprinkled with chaat masala.

Note:

- When skewering delicate meats like fish, prawns and vegetables, it is advisable to use **thinner skewers,** then there is less chance of the vegetable or fish to break.

- The temperature should be **low moderate** as even a little high temperature makes the sea food tough.

Vegetables

Shahi Malai Kofta

Serves 6

150 gm paneer (cottage cheese) - grated
2 small boiled potatoes - grated, 2 tbsp finely chopped poodina (mint)
2 tbsp maida
½ tsp garam masala, ¼ tsp red chilli powder, ¾ tsp salt, or to taste
2-3 tbsp maida (plain flour) - to coat

GRAVY

2 onion - ground to a paste
2 tbsp magaz (water melon seeds)
2 tbsp kaju - soaked in warm water
4 tbsp curd
½ cup malai or cream - mixed with ½ cup milk
2 tbsp desi ghee or butter or 3 tbsp oil
1 tsp garam masala, ¾ tsp red chilli powder
1 tsp kasoori methi (dry fenugreek leaves), 1 tsp salt, or to taste
3 chhoti illaichi (green cardamoms) - crushed to a powder

FILLING
½ onion - very finely chopped
½" piece ginger - very finely chopped
4-5 kajus (cashews) - chopped
¼ tsp each of salt, red chilli powder, garam masala

GARNISH
1 tsp magaz seeds (watermelon seeds) - roasted on a tawa (gridle) and fresh
coriander leaves

1. To prepare the koftas, mix grated paneer, potatoes, poodina, red chilli powder, salt, garam masala and 2 tbsp maida. Mix well till smooth. Make 12 balls.

2. For the filling, heat 2 tsp ghee. Add onions and ginger. Fry till golden brown. Add kaju, salt, garam masala and chilli powder. Remove from fire.

3. Flatten each ball of paneer mixture, put 1 tsp of onion filling in each ball. Form a ball again. Roll each ball in a maida. Dust to remove excess maida.

4. Deep fry 1-2 koftas at a time in medium hot oil. Keep aside.
5. Soak kaju and magaz in water for 10 minutes. Drain and grind to a very fine paste with curd.
6. Heat ghee. Add grated onion. Cook on low flame till it turns transparent and ghee separates. Do not let it turn brown by keeping on high flame.
7. Add kaju – magaz paste. Cook for 2-3 minutes on low flame. Add garam masala, red chilli powder and salt.
8. Add cream. Stir. Mix well. Add kasoori methi and stir for 2 minutes.
9. Add 1½ cups water to thin down the gravy. Boil on low heat for 1 minute.
10. At the time of serving, add powdered chhoti illaichi and boil the gravy. Add koftas and simmer on low heat for 1 minute. Serve garnished with a swirl of cream, roasted magaz and fresh coriander leaves.

Variation:

Whole mushroom sauted in butter, small potatoes boiled and deep fried, boiled corn and peas, Navrattan Curry (mixed vegetables, paneer and tinned pineapple) etc. can be used with this gravy.

Phool Dilkhush

Pan fried whole cauliflowers coated with a delicious masala and topped with green peas.

Serves 4

2 very small whole cauliflowers

MASALA
4 tbsp oil
3 onions - ground to a paste
3 tomatoes - roughly chopped
1" ginger - chopped
seeds of 1 moti illaichi
3-4 saboot kali mirch (peppercorns) and 2 laung (cloves)
2 tbsp curd - beat well till smooth
½ tsp red chilli powder
½ tsp garam masala
½ tsp haldi, ½ tsp amchoor
½ tsp salt, or to taste

Mutton Seekh: Recipe on page 18 ➤

TO GARNISH
¼ cup boiled peas

1. Remove stems of cauliflowers. Boil 6 cups water with 2 tsp salt. Put the whole cauliflowers in it. When the water starts to boil again, remove from fire. Leave them in hot water for 10 minutes. Remove from water and refresh in cold water. Wipe dry on a clean kitchen towel.
2. Heat 5-6 tbsp oil in a large flat kadhai or a pan. Put both cauliflowers with flower side down in oil. Cover and cook on medium flame, stirring occasionally till the cauliflowers turn golden and get patches of dark brown colour here and there. Remove from oil. Keep aside.
3. Heat ½ tbsp oil in a clean kadhai. Add moti illaichi, saboot kali mirch and laung. After a minute add chopped tomatoes and ginger. Cook for 4-5 minutes till they turn soft. Grind the cooked tomatoes to a paste.
4. Heat 3½ tbsp oil. Add onion paste. Cook till onions turn golden brown.
5. Add tomato paste. Cook for 3-4 minutes on low flame till masala turns dry.
6. Add well beaten curd. Cook till masala turns reddish again.

7. Reduce heat. Add red chilli powder, garam masala, haldi, amchoor and salt. Cook for 1 minute. Add ¼ cup water to get a thick, dry masala. Boil. Cook for 1 minute on low flame. Remove from fire.

8. Insert a little masala in between the florets of the fried cauliflower, especially from the backside.

9. To serve, arrange the cauliflowers on a platter. Add ¼ cup water to the masala to make it a masala gravy. Boil. Add ½ tsp salt or to taste. Pour over the arranged cauliflowers. Heat in a microwave or a preheated oven. Alternately, heat the cauliflower in a kadhai in 1 tbsp oil at the time of serving. Heat the masala gravy separately. Arrange the heated cauliflowers on a serving platter. Pour the hot masala gravy over it.

10. Sprinkle some boiled peas on it and on the sides. Serve.

Paalak Chaman

Serves 4

250 gms paalak (spinach) - chopped (2½ cups)
a pinch of sugar
4 tbsp kasoori methi (dry fenugreek leaves)
200 gm paneer - cut into ¼" cubes and deep fried
2 tbsp cashewnuts (kaju) - soaked in warm water for 20 minutes and ground to a
paste
½" stick dalchini (cinnamon)
2 chhoti illaichi (green cardamoms)
3-4 laung (cloves)
2 tbsp oil
2 onions - ground to a paste
1/3 cup malai or cream
salt to taste
a pinch of sugar

BAGHAR/CHOWK(TEMPERING)
1 tbsp desi ghee, ½ tsp red chilli powder

1. Boil spinach in ½ cup water with a pinch of sugar. Cover and cook on low flame for 4-5 minutes till spinach turns soft. Remove from fire. Cool and blend to a puree.
2. Fry tiny pieces of paneer till golden brown.
3. Crush dalchini, laung and seeds of chhoti illaichi to a rough powder. Keep aside.
4. Grind cashewnuts separately with a little water to a paste.
5. Heat oil. Add onions and cook on low heat till oil separates and they turn light brown.
6. Add the freshly ground masala. Cook for a few seconds.
7. Add the kasoori methi and paalak. Bhuno for 5-7 minutes till dry.
8. Add malai or cream, cook on low heat for 3-4 minutes.
9. Add the fried paneer.
10. Add cashewnut paste and cook for a few seconds.
11. Add salt and sugar to taste. Simmer for a few minutes.
12. To serve, heat 1 tbsp desi ghee for the baghar. Remove from fire. Add red chilli powder to it and pour over paalak. Serve immediately.

Arbi Ajwaini

Arbi combined with a masala of onion rings flavoured with carom seeds.

Serves 4

½ kg arbi (colocasia)
2 onions - cut into rings
½" piece ginger - chopped finely
2-3 green chillies - cut into thin long pieces
¼ tsp haldi
2 tomatoes - chopped
1 tsp ajwain (carom seeds)
½ tsp jeera (cumin seeds)
1 tsp dhania (coriander) powder
½ tsp salt, or to taste
½ tsp red chilli powder
½ tsp amchoor (dried mango powder)
½ cup chopped coriander

1. Pressure cook arbi with 3 cups water and 2 tsp salt to give one whistle. Keep on low flame for 4 minutes. Do not over boil. Peel and flatten each piece between the palms.
2. Heat 2 cups oil in a kadhai for frying. Put 4-5 pieces of flattened arbi at one time in oil. Fry till golden brown. Remove from oil. Keep aside.
3. Heat 2 tbsp oil in a clean kadhai. Reduce flame. Add ajwain and jeera. Cook till jeera turns golden.
4. Add onion rings and cook till soft. Add haldi and mix.
5. Add tomatoes and cook for 2 minutes till soft. Add ginger and stir for a minute.
6. Add chilli powder, amchoor, salt and dhania powder. Stir to mix well. Add 2-3 tbsp water. Boil.
7. Add fried arbi. Mix well.
8. Add hara dhania and green chillies. Stir fry for 2 minutes.

Note: If the arbi is not boiled in salted water, add a little extra salt.

Dal Makhani

Serves 6

1 cup urad saboot (whole black beans)
1 tbsp ghee or oil
5 cups of water
1½ tsp salt
3 tbsp ghee or oil
4 tomatoes - pureed in a grinder
½ tsp garam masala
1 tbsp kasoori methi (dry fenugreek leaves)
2 tsp tomato ketchup
2-3 tbsp butter, ½ cup milk, ½ cup cream
a pinch of jaiphal (nutmeg) - grated

GRIND TO A PASTE
2 dry, whole red chillies, preferably Kashmiri red chillies - deseeded & soaked
for 10 minutes and then drained
1" piece ginger, 5-6 flakes garlic

1. Pressure cook dal with 5 cups water, 1 tbsp ghee, salt and half of the the ginger-garlic-chilli paste.
2. After the first whistle, keep on low flame for 40 minutes. Remove from fire. After the pressure drops, mash the hot dal a little. Keep aside.
3. Heat ghee. Add tomatoes pureed in a grinder. Cook until thick and dry.
4. Add the garam masala. Cook until ghee separates.
5. Add kasoori methi and the left over ginger-garlic-chilli paste. Cook further for 1-2 minutes.
6. Add this tomato mixture to the boiled dal. Add tomato ketchup also.
7. Add butter. Simmer on low flame for 15-20 minutes, stirring and mashing the dal occasionally with a karchhi against the sides of the cooker.
8. Add milk. Mix very well with a karcchi. Simmer for 10 minutes more, to get the right colour and smoothness.
9. Reduce heat. Add jaiphal. Mix. Add cream gradually, stirring continuously. Remove from fire. Serve.

Note: Originally the dal was cooked by leaving it overnight on the burning coal angithis. The longer the dal simmered, the better it tasted.

Paneer Makhani

Serves 4

250 gm paneer - cut into 1" cubes
5 large (500 gm) tomatoes - each cut into 4 pieces
2 tbsp desi ghee or butter and 2 tbsp oil
4-5 flakes garlic and 1" piece ginger - ground to a paste
1 tbsp kasoori methi (dried fenugreek leaves), 1 tsp tomato ketchup
½ tsp jeera (cumin seeds), 2 tsp dhania powder, ½ tsp garam masala
1 tsp salt, or to taste, ½ tsp red chilli powder, preferably degi mirch
½-1 cup milk, approx., ½ cup cream (optional), ½ cup water

CASHEW PASTE

3 tbsp kaju - soaked in ¼ cup warm water for 15 minutes and ground to a paste

TADKA/CHOWK/TEMPERING

1 tbsp oil, ½ tsp rai, 3-4 tbsp curry leaves, a pinch of red chilli powder

1. Boil tomatoes in ½ cup water. Simmer for 4-5 minutes on low heat till tomatoes turn soft. Remove from fire and cool. Grind the tomatoes along with the water to a smooth puree.

2. Heat oil and ghee or butter in a kadhai. Reduce heat. Add jeera. When it turns golden, add ginger-garlic paste.
3. When paste starts to change colour add the above tomato puree and cook till absolutely dry.
4. Add kasoori methi and tomato ketchup.
5. Add masalas - dhania powder, garam masala, salt and red chilli powder. Mix well for a few seconds. Cook till oil separates.
6. Add cashew paste. Mix well for 2 minutes.
7. Add water. Boil. Simmer on low heat for 4-5 minutes. Reduce heat.
8. Add the paneer cubes. Keep aside to cool for about 5 minutes.
9. Add milk to the cold paneer masala to get a thick curry, mix gently. (Remember to add milk only after the masala is no longer hot, to prevent the milk from curdling. After adding milk, heat curry on low heat.)
10. Heat on low heat, stirring continuously till just about to boil.
11. Add cream, keeping the heat very low and stirring continuously. Remove from fire immediately and transfer to a serving dish.
12. For chowk, heat oil. Add rai. After 30 seconds add curry leaves. Stir.
13. Remove from fire. Add chilli powder & pour over the hot gravy.

Anjeeri Gobhi

Picture on page 103   *Serves 6*

Fried cauliflower, cooked in an anjeer flavoured masala.

1 medium cauliflower (gobhi) - cut into medium size florets with long stalks
1 tsp jeera (cumin seeds)
2 onions - chopped
1 tsp chopped ginger
1 tsp chopped garlic
2 green chillies - deseeded & chopped

ANJEER PASTE
8 small anjeers (figs)
1 cup dahi (yogurt)
1 tsp garam masala
¾ tsp red chilli powder
1¾ tsp salt or to taste

TO SPRINKLE
2 small anjeers (figs) - chopped and roasted on a tawa (gridle)

1. Break the cauliflower into medium florets, keeping the stalk intact.
2. Heat 1 cup oil in a kadhai. Add all the cauliflower pieces and fry to a golden colour. Remove from oil and keep aside.
3. Churn all the ingredients given under anjeer paste in a mixer till smooth.
4. Heat 2 tbsp oil in a kadhai. Add jeera. When it turns golden, add chopped onions. Stir till light brown.
5. Add ginger, garlic and green chillies. Cook for a minute.
6. Add the prepared anjeer paste. Stir-fry for 2-3 minutes till the curd dries up a little. Keep aside till serving time.
7. Chop finely 2 anjeers and roast on a tawa till fragrant. Keep aside.

Step 7

8. At serving time, heat the masala and add fried cauliflower. Mix well.
    Sprinkle roasted anjeer on top. Serve hot.

41

Vegetable Korma

Curd, coconut and cashews form the base of a good korma. A little cream (¼-½ cup) can be added at the time of serving.

Picture on page 1   *Serves 4*

½ cup shelled peas, 2 small carrots - cut into round slices
6 french beans - cut into ½" diagonal pieces
6-8 small florets (1" pieces) of cauliflower - fried till golden and cooked
1-2 small slices of tinned pineapple - cut into 1" pieces, optional (see note)
½ cup cream

GRIND TOGETHER TO A PASTE

3 tbsp cashews (kaju) - soaked in warm water for 10 minutes and drained
¾ cup curd, 2 tbsp grated coconut (fresh or desiccated)
½" piece ginger, 3-4 flakes garlic
2 tsp dhania saboot (coriander seeds), seeds of 2-3 chhoti illaichi

OTHER INGREDIENTS

2 onions - chopped finely
¼ tsp haldi (turmeric) powder, ½ tsp garam masala, 2 tsp salt

1. Soak kaju in warm water for 10 minutes. Drain. Grind them with all the ingredients given under paste.
2. Heat 4 tbsp oil. Add onions. Cook till onions turn golden brown.
3. Add haldi. Stir to mix well.
4. Add the cashew-curd paste. Cook on low heat for 3-4 minutes.
5. Add salt and garam masala. Stir for a few seconds.
6. Add french beans, peas and carrots. Stir for 2 minutes.
7. Add 1½-2 cups of water or enough to get a thick gravy. Boil. Simmer covered for 8-10 minutes till the vegetables get done. Keep aside.
8. At the time of serving, add cauliflower and pineapple. Boil for 1 minute.
9. Reduce heat. Add ceam and immediately remove from fire. Serve sprinkled with chopped coriander.

Note:

- The left over pineapple can be stored in a steel or plastic box in the freezer compartment of the refrigerator without getting spoilt.

- If using fresh pineapple, cut into pieces and cook in a little water for 7-8 minutes till soft. Do not use it without cooking, as the gravy may turn bitter.

Gajar Paneer Jalfrezi

Paneer deliciously combined with carrots to make a semi dry vegetable.

Picture on back cover   Serves 4-5

200 gm paneer - cut into thin long pieces
250 gms (3-4) carrots - cut diagonally into very thin slices
1 long, firm tomato - cut into 4, pulp removed and cut into thin long pieces
15-20 curry leaves
4 tbsp oil

COLLECT TOGETHER
½ tsp jeera (cumin seeds)
½ tsp sarson (mustard seeds)
¾ tsp kalonji (½ tsp plus ¼ tsp) (onion seeds)
¼ tsp methi daana (fenugreek seeds)

MIX TOGETHER
5 tbsp tomato puree
2 tbsp tomato ketchup
2 tsp ginger-garlic paste or 2 tsp ginger-garlic - finely chopped

½ tsp red chilli powder
½ tsp amchoor powder, 1¼ tsp dhania powder
1 tsp salt, or to taste

1. Mix together - tomato puree, tomato ketchup, ginger, garlic, red chilli powder, dhania powder, amchoor and salt in a bowl. Keep aside.
2. Heat 3 tbsp oil in a kadhai. Add the collected seeds together. When jeera turns golden, reduce heat and add curry leaves and stir for a few seconds.
3. Add the tomato puree mixed with dry masalas and stir on low heat for 2 minutes.
4. Add carrots. Stir for 2-3 minutes.
5. Add ¼ cup water. Cover the kadhai. Cook on low heat for about 4-5 minutes, till carrot is tender, but still remains crunchy at the same time.
6. Add paneer and tomato slices. Stir till well blended. Remove from fire.

Note: 1 capsicum can also be added to add colour to the dish. Add capsicum cut into thin fingers after the carrot is done. Saute capsicum for a minute and then add the paneer.

Cheesy Broccoli Koftas

Picture on facing page   *Serves 4-6*

1 medium broccoli - grated finely along with tender stalks (2 cups grated)
1 potato - boiled and grated
2 tbsp roasted peanuts (moongphali) - crushed coarsely
¼ tsp coarsely crushed saboot kali mirch (peppercorns)
½ tsp salt, ¼ tsp garam masala, ¼ tsp amchoor
1½ tbsp cornflour, a pinch of baking powder
1 cheese cube (20 gm) - cut into 10 pieces, ½ tbsp butter

GRAVY
3 tbsp oil
1 cup tomato puree
1 tsp jeera (cumin seeds)
1" piece ginger - grated, 1 tsp ginger paste, 4 tbsp chopped coriander
1¼ tsp salt, ¾ tsp garam masala, 1½ tsp dhania powder, ½ tsp red chilli pd.
1 cup water, 1 cup milk
¼-½ cup cream or fresh malai

1. Grate the broccoli florets and the tender stems very finely.
2. Heat butter in a pan. Add chopped broccoli. Add ¼ tsp salt. Stir on medium heat for 3-4 minutes on low heat. Remove from heat.
3. Grate the potato well. Add peanuts, salt, crushed peppercorns, garam masala, amchoor, cornflour, baking powder and cooked broccoli to the potato.
4. Make balls of the potato-broccoli mixture.
5. Flatten a ball and put a small piece of cheese in it. Make a ball again.
6. Deep fry 2-3 balls at a time till golden. Drain on absorbent paper.
7. To prepare the gravy, heat oil. Add jeera. Let it turn golden.
8. When golden, add ginger shreds and paste. Stir for a few seconds.
9. Add tomato puree. Reduce heat. Add salt, garam masala, dhania powder and red chilli. Cook for 5 minutes, till puree turns dry. Add chopped coriander, mix. Add enough water to get a thick gravy. Boil. Cook on low heat for 4-5 minutes. Remove from fire. Let it cool down.
10. To serve, add enough milk to the cold gravy stirring continuously. Add koftas. Keep on low heat and stir continuously till just about to boil. Add cream and remove from fire after 2-3 seconds. Serve.

Achaari Bhindi

An unusual combination of pickle spices masala and bhindi. Do give it a try.

Serves 4   *Picture on page 103*

½ kg bhindi
4 big (300 gms) tomatoes - chopped finely
2 tsp ginger or garlic paste
15-20 curry leaves
½ tsp haldi
½ tsp red chilli powder
1 tsp dhania powder
¾ tsp salt, or to taste

COLLECT TOGETHER
a pinch of hing (asafoetida)
1 tsp saunf (fennel)
½ tsp kalonji (onion seeds)
¼ tsp methi dana (fenugreek seeds)
½ tsp rai (mustard seeds)

1. Wash bhindi and wipe dry. Cut the tip of the head of each bhindi, leaving the pointed end as it is. Now cut the bhindi vertically from the middle making 2 smaller pieces from each bhindi. Heat oil in a kadhai and deep fry the bhindi on medium heat in 2 batches. Do not over fry the bhindi, it should retain it's green colour. Drain on a paper napkin. Keep aside.

2. Heat 2 tbsp oil and add ginger or garlic paste. Add curry patta and stir fry for a minute.

3. Add all collected ingredients. Stir till methi dana turns brown.

4. Add haldi, chilli powder, dhania powder & salt. Stir for 30 seconds.

5. Add chopped tomatoes and stir for about 7-8 minutes or till oil separates.

6. Add fried bhindi. Sprinkle ¼ tsp salt and stir gently on slow fire for a few minutes till well mixed. Serve hot.

Chicken, Mutton & Fish

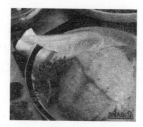

Malai Gosht

Delicious mutton in a creamy, white gravy. Ideal for a party.

Serves 4-5

500 gms boneless mutton - cut into 1½" pieces
3 tbsp butter
3 tbsp oil
2 tsp ginger-garlic paste
¾ tsp salt or to taste, ½ tsp red chilli powder
½ tsp garam masala
4 tbsp cashews (kaju), ground to a paste with 4 tbsp curd
4 tbsp kasoori methi (dry fenugreek leaves)
1 cup thin fresh cream
½ cup milk
1 tbsp chopped mint (poodina)

GRIND TO A PASTE IN A MIXER
2 onions

CRUSH SPICES TOGETHER
½ stick dalchini (cinnamon)
seeds of 2-3 chhoti illaichi (green cardamom)
3-4 laung (cloves)
4-5 saboot kali mirch (peppercorns)

1. Grind onions to a paste in a mixer.
2. Crush whole spices together.
3. In a pressure cooker put mutton with salt, ground spices and onion paste with 3 cups of water. Pressure cook on high flame for 7 minutes. Reduce heat and cook further for 5 minutes. Remove from fire. Let the pressure drop. Strain and keep stock aside.
4. Heat butter and oil together. Add ginger-garlic. Mix. Add mutton pieces, leaving behind the stock and bhuno on medium heat till golden. Add all masalas, stock, kaju paste and kasoori methi. Cook covered for 5-7 minutes on low heat, stirring in between.
5. Reduce heat. Add cream and milk on low heat. Cook uncovered for 2-3 minutes, stirring in between. Remove from fire. Sprinkle some chopped mint leaves, serve hot.

Saag Wala Meat

Lamb cooked in spinach mildly flavoured with green cardamoms.

Serves 4-5

750 gm mutton (lamb)
1 kg spinach - shredded or chopped finely
6-8 tbsp oil
4 chhoti illaichi (green cardamoms) - powdered
2 onions - chopped finely
1½ tbsp ginger-garlic paste
½ cup thick curd
1 tsp salt, or to taste
1 tsp red chilli powder
½ tsp garam masala

1. Chop the spinach leaves, discarding stems. Wash in several changes of water. Strain and keep aside.
2. Heat oil in a pressure cooker. Add chhoti illaichi. Wait for a few seconds.

3. Add ginger, garlic pastes and stir for 1 minute. Add onions and cook till onions turn light brown.
4. Add mutton and bhuno for 10-12 minutes till the mutton turns golden brown and all the water evaporates.
5. Add salt and red chilli powder. Add curd and stir.
6. Add the spinach and stir for 1-2 minutes.
7. Add 1½ cups of water and pressure cook for 7 minutes on high flame after the pressure forms and then for 5 minutes on low flame. Remove from fire.
8. Let the pressure drop by itself. Open the lid and bhuno again till all the moisture evaporates and the saag coats the mutton well.
9. Add garam masala and serve hot garnished with 1 tbsp of cream and ginger matchsticks. Serve hot with nan or lachha parantha.

Murg Achaari

Picture on facing page   Serves 5-6

1 chicken (800 gm) - cut into 12 pieces
10 tbsp mustard oil
2 large onions - chopped finely or grated
4 tbsp ginger - garlic paste
1 tsp haldi powder, 2 tsp salt, 2 tsp sugar
2 tsp red chilli powder (Kashmiri)
1 cup curd - well beaten
4 tbsp lemon juice
some fresh dhania for garnishing

COLLECT TOGETHER
8-10 laung (cloves)
5-6 chhoti illaichi (green cardamoms)
1 tsp shah jeera (black cumin)
1 tsp methi dana (fenugreek seeds), ½ tsp kalaunji (onion seeds)
2 tsp rai (mustard seeds), a pinch of hing (asafoetida)
5-6 whole, dry red chillies

1. Heat mustard oil till it smokes. Remove from fire and cool.
2. Heat oil again. Add all the collected spices - laung, chhoti illaichi, shah jeera, methi seeds, kalaunji, rai, hing and 5-6 whole, dry red chillies. Fry for ½ minute till methi dana turns golden.
3. Add onions and fry till golden brown.
4. Add ginger and garlic paste. Fry for 1-2 minutes.
5. Add chicken, salt, haldi, sugar & red chilli powder. Fry for 3-4 minutes on high flame.
6. Add well beaten curd. Keep stirring till it boils. Cook, stirring all the time for another 2 minutes.
7. Cover, lower heat and cook for 12-15 minutes or till chicken is tender.
8. Add lemon juice. Give 1-2 boils. Add ¼ cup water if you like and give 2-3 boils.
9. Serve hot, garnished with fresh dhania.

Note: Paneer or Dum aloo made in this way is also very delicious.

Butter Chicken

An all time favourite!

Serves 4

1 medium sized chicken (800 gm) - cut into 12 pieces
juice of 1 lemon
½ tsp chilli powder, 1¼ tsp salt, or to taste

MARINADE

1 cup curd - hang for 30 minutes in a muslin cloth
2 tbsp thick malai or 2 tbsp cream
1 tbsp garlic paste, 1 tsp ginger paste
1 tbsp kasoori methi (dry fenugreek leaves)
few drops of orange red colour
½ tsp kala namak, 1 tsp garam masala

MAKHANI GRAVY

½ kg (6-7) tomatoes - blanched, peeled and ground to a very smooth puree or
2 cups readymade tomato puree
2 tbsp butter
2-3 tbsp oil, 1 tej patta (bay leaf), 2 tbsp ginger-garlic paste

Contd...

¼ tsp Kashmiri laal mirch or degi mirch, 1 tsp tandoori masala
1 cup milk, 2 tbsp cream, ½ tsp garam masala, ¼ tsp sugar or to taste

PASTE
4 tbsp kaju (cashewnuts) - soaked in hot water for 15 minutes, drained and
ground to a very fine paste with a little water

1. Wash, and pat dry the chicken. Rub lemon juice, salt and chilli powder on chicken and keep aside for ½ hour.
2. For the marinade, mix curd, malai, garlic and ginger paste, kasoori methi, kala namak, garam masala and colour. Rub the chicken with this mixture. Keep aside for 3-4 hours in the fridge.
3. Heat the gas tandoor (flame should be minimum) or oven to 180°C. Place the chicken on the grill or wire rack (in the oven place a tray covered with aluminium foil, underneath the chicken to collect the drippings). Grill for 15 minutes.
4. Pour some oil with a spoon on all pieces. Turn pieces & grill for another 10-15 minutes, till the chicken is dry and well cooked. Be careful not to make the chicken blackish and burnt. Keep tandoori chicken aside.

5. To prepare the makhani gravy, boil water in a pan. Add tomatoes to boiling water. Boil for 3-4 minutes. Remove from water and peel. Grind to a smooth puree. Keep aside.

6. Heat butter and oil together in a non stick pan or a kadhai. Add tej patta. Stir for a few seconds. Add ginger and garlic paste, cook until liquid evaporates and the paste just changes colour.

7. Add pureed tomatoes or readymade puree, degi mirch and sugar. Cook until the puree turns very dry and fat separates.

8. Add cashew paste, stir for a few seconds on medium heat till fat separates. Lower the heat. Add about 1 cup of water to get the desired gravy. Bring to a boil, stirring constantly.

9. Add tandoori chicken and salt. Cover and simmer for 5-7 minutes till the gravy turns to a bright colour. Reduce heat. Add milk on very low heat and bring to a boil, stirring continuously. Keep stirring for 1-2 minutes on low heat till you get the desired thickness of the gravy.

10. Remove from fire. Add cream, stirring continuously. Add garam masala and tandoori masala. Serve garnished with some cream.

Note: For tandoori chicken, if you do not have a tandoor or an oven, simply marinate chicken & cook in a kadhai with 5 tbsp butter till done.

Kasoori Murg Malai

Curd and cream form the base of this white gravy with a fragrant flavour of fenugreek.

Serves 5-6

1 chicken (800 gm) - cut into 12 pieces or 500 gm boneless - cut into 2" pieces
1 cup curd - hang for ½ hour in a muslin cloth and then beat till smooth
150 ml (1 cup) fresh cream
1 tbsp kasoori methi (dried fenugreek leaves)
6 tbsp oil
1 tsp garam masala
1½ tsp salt, or to taste
1 tsp white pepper (adjust to taste)

GRIND TOGETHER
2 medium onions
6 flakes garlic
1" piece ginger
1-2 green chillies

1. Grind together onions, green chillies, garlic and ginger with a little water to a fine paste.
2. Heat oil. Add onion paste and fry till it just starts to change colour. Do not make it brown.
3. Add chicken, salt, garam masala and white pepper. Fry for 3-4 minutes on moderate heat till chicken changes colour.
4. Add hung curd and kasoori methi. Mix well and cook for 3-4 minutes.
5. Cover, lower heat and cook till chicken is tender, approximately for 15-20 minutes.
6. Add ½ cup water and bring to a boil. Simmer for 2-3 minutes to get a thick masala gravy.
7. Keeping the heat low, add fresh cream. Mix well and give one boil, stirring continuously on low heat.
8. Serve hot garnished with kasoori methi and fresh dhania.

Murg Kadhai Waala

Serves 4- 6

1 medium sized (800 gms) chicken - cut into 12 pieces or 500 gm boneless
chicken - cut into bite size pieces

1½ tsp saboot dhania (coriander seeds) - roasted lightly and coarsely crushed

6 tbsp oil

½ tsp methi dana (fenugreek seeds), 3-4 whole, dry red chillies

3 large onions - cut into slices

15-20 flakes garlic - crushed & chopped

4 large tomatoes - chopped, ½ cup tomato puree (8 tbsp)

1¾ tsp salt, or to taste

3-4 tbsp kasoori methi (dry fenugreek leaves)

1 tsp red chilli powder, 1¼ tsp dhania powder (ground coriander)

4-5 tbsp cream, 1½ cups milk

½ cup chopped green coriander

1- 2 capsicum - cut into very thin long pieces

2" piece ginger - cut into match sticks

1-2 green chillies - cut into thin long slices

1. Dry roast saboot dhania (coriander seeds) on a tawa lightly. Do not make them brown. Pound them on a chakla-belan (rolling board & pin) to split the seeds. Keep aside.
2. Heat oil in a kadhai. Reduce heat. Add methi dana and whole red chillies and stir for a few seconds till methi dana turns golden.
3. Add onion and cook on medium heat till light brown.
4. Add garlic and stir for 1 minute.
5. Add tomatoes. Cook for 2 minutes. Add kasoori methi.
6. Add the saboot dhania, red chilli powder and dhania powder.
7. Add chicken and bhuno for 4-5 minutes on medium high flame, stirring well to mix everything together.
8. Add salt. Cover & cook for 10-15 minutes till tender, stirring occasionally.
9. Add tomato puree and chopped coriander. Cook for 3-4 minutes or till dry.
10. Reduce heat. Add milk and cook for 2-3 minutes on slow fire, stirring continuously.
11. Add capsicum, ginger match sticks and green chilli slices. Mix well.
12. Keeping the heat low, add cream. Mix well & remove from fire. Serve

Meat Khada Masala

Serves 6-8

1 kg mutton

¾ cup ghee

4 onions - chopped, 5 tbsp garlic - chopped, 5 tbsp ginger - chopped

5 green chillies - chopped

4 tomatoes - chopped

2 cups yogurt - beat till smooth

2 tsp salt or to taste

KHADHA MASALAS

3 moti illaichi (black cardamoms)

5-6 chhoti illaichi (green cardamoms)

6 laung (cloves)

1" stick dalchini (cinnamon)

1 tej patta (bay leaf)

2-3 blades javetri (mace)

CRUSHED OR POUNDED MASALAS
2½ tsp saboot dhania (coriander seeds) - pounded or crushed coarsely
3-4 dry, red chillies - pounded or crushed coarsely
10-15 saboot kali mirch (peppercorns) - pounded
1 tsp shah jeera (black cumin) - powdered

1. Heat ghee in a pressure cooker. Collect all khada masalas together and add to hot oil. Saute over medium heat for a minute till it begins to crackle.
2. Add onions and cook till golden brown. Add garlic, ginger and green chillies. Stir for a few minutes.
3. Add mutton pieces and the pounded masalas.
4. Bhuno till the mutton pieces are brown, for about 7-8 minutes.
5. Lower the heat add the yogurt and bhuno for 8-10 minutes.
6. Add the tomatoes and salt. Bhuno till the masala leaves ghee.
7. Add 2½ cups of water and pressure cook for 7 minutes on high flame when pressure forms and then for 5 minutes on low flame. Remove from fire and let the pressure drop by itself.
8. Sprinkle garam masala and coriander.
9. Garnish with slit green chillies. Serve with naan or parantha.

Chicken Chettinad

The fiery curry of Chettinad - a place in South India. Though it is a hot curry, yet it has a wonderful flavour. The peppercorns impart the flavour to the dish.

Serves 4-6

1 chicken (700-800 gm) - cut into 12 pieces
5-6 tbsp oil, 1 large onion - chopped very finely
¼ cup curry patta
3 tomatoes - pureed, 1 tsp salt, or to taste, 2-3 tbsp lemon juice
2-3" piece ginger, 8-10 flakes garlic
1 tbsp khus khus (poppy seeds)
2 tbsp kaju tukda (cashewnuts)
1 cup milk

CHETTINAD MASALA

½ cup freshly grated coconut (remove brown skin before grating)
1 tsp saboot dhania (coriander seeds)
½ tsp jeera (cumin seeds), 2½ tsp saboot kali mirch (peppercorns)
5-6 dry, red chillies, 3 chhoti illaichi (green cardamoms)
2-3 laung (cloves), 1" stick dalchini (cinnamon stick)

1. Soak khus khus and kaju in a little warm water for 10-15 minutes.
2. Heat 1 tbsp oil in a pan or tawa. Add coconut, saboot dhania, jeera, saunf, red chillies, laung, dalchini and seeds of chhoti illaichi to oil and stir-fry till fragrant. Remove from fire.
3. Drain khus and cashews. Grind together the roasted masala with the drained khus-khus-cashewnuts, ginger and garlic to a smooth paste in a mixer grinder to a very smooth paste with ¼ cup water.
4. Heat oil in a kadhai and add the chopped onions. Fry till light brown.
5. Add the pureed tomatoes, salt, haldi and chilli powder. Cook till tomatoes are well blended with the masala and oil separates.
6. Add chicken and cook or bhuno for 7-10 minutes or till almost cooked.
7. Add the ground paste and curry leaves. Saute for 2 minutes.
8. Add lemon juice and 1½ cups of water. Cover and cook till chicken is tender, stirring in between. Cook till the masala is thick. Keep aside till serving time.
9. At serving time, add 1 cup milk to the chicken. Keep on low heat, stirring continuously, till it boils. Serve garnished with coriander.

Rogan Josh

A spicy, thin mutton curry, cooked with saunf & saunth.

Serves 4

½ kg mutton (lamb)
½ cup thick curd
½ tsp hing powder
3-4 saboot kali mirch (peppercorns)
1" stick dalchini (cinnamon)
6 tbsp oil

GRIND TOGETHER & SIEVE TO GET A FINE POWDER
1 tsp ginger powder (saunth)
1½ tsp saunf (fennel)
seeds of 3 moti illaichi (brown cardamoms)
½ tsp jeera (cumin seeds)
2-3 laung (cloves)
2-3 dry, red chillies, salt to taste
½ tsp degi mirch (red chilli powder)

1. Wash and pat dry mutton on a kitchen towel.
2. Heat oil in a pressure cooker. Add hing, dalchini and saboot kali mirch.
3. Add dry meat and stir fry for 4-5 minutes or till the mutton turns dry, golden brown and gives a well fried look. There should be no water of the meat left.
4. Mix the curd with the sifted powdered masala and add it to the mutton. Add salt. Stir fry for 5-7 minutes till the curd blends well and turns dry.
5. Add 2 cups of water, pressure cook to give 2-3 whistles. Reduce flame and cook for 4 minutes. Check for tenderness.
6. Serve hot with roomali roti.

Achaari Korma

Serves 6-8

1 kg mutton (boneless) - cut into 1" botis
½ tsp haldi (turmeric)
2 tsp salt, or to taste
4 tsp mustard oil, ½ cup ghee
2 onions - sliced
8 whole, dry red chillies
1 tsp sarson or rai (mustard seeds), 5 laung (cloves)
a pinch of hing (asafoetida)
1 tsp jeera (cumin seeds)
1 tsp kalonji (onion seeds)
1 tsp red chilli powder
2 tsp gur (jaggery) powder
4 tsp ginger - chopped, 3 tsp garlic - chopped
1½ cups yoghurt - beat well till smooth
2 tbsp lemon juice

1. In a pressure cooker put the mutton with salt, haldi and 6 cups of water. Pressure cook on high flame for 7 minutes after the pressure forms. Reduce heat and cook further for 5 minutes. Remove from fire. Let the pressure drop. Strain and keep the stock aside.
2. Heat mustard oil in kadhai till it starts to smoke. Remove from fire and add ghee. Return to fire and add onions and fry till golden brown. Remove the onions and keep aside for garnishing.
3. In the same oil add whole red chillies and fry until black. Remove and discard the chillies.
4. Reheat this oil (chilli oil). Add rai, laung, hing, jeera and kalaunji. Saute until the seeds begin to crackle or till jeera turns golden.
5. Add the cooked lamb, 1 tsp red chilli powder, gur, ginger and garlic.
6. Bhuno for 15 minutes till the mutton becomes brownish in colour. Add the reserved stock and lemon juice. Simmer for 2-3 minutes.
7. Remove the kadhai from the fire and add the yogurt. This prevents the yogurt from curdling. Mix well and bhuno on medium flame until the oil leaves the masala. Adjust the seasoning.
8. Put in a serving dish and garnish with fried onions. Serve hot.

Fish in Goan Curry

This spicy hot curry goes by the name of just Goan curry. It is a traditional fish curry which is included in most of their meals. Traditionally the fish is not deep fried, but I found the recipe better by frying the fish.

Picture on page 2   *Serves 4*

½ kg boneless fish, preferably Sole - cut into 1½" pieces
3 tbsp dry besan (gramflour), 2 tbsp lemon juice, 1 tsp garlic paste
½ tsp salt and ½ tsp pepper

GRIND TO A PASTE
½ cup + 2 tbsp coconut - grated freshly
8 dry red chillies, 1 tsp jeera (cumin seeds)
1 tbsp saboot dhania (coriander seeds), a pinch of haldi (turmeric powder)
3 tbsp imli (tamarind) - deseeded
1" piece ginger, 5-6 flakes garlic

BATTER
½ cup besan, 3 tbsp chopped coriander
½ tsp each of salt, garam masala & pepper

Chicken Lollipops: Recipe on page 84 ➤

OTHER INGREDIENTS
4-5 tbsp oil
1 onion - chopped, 2 tomatoes - chopped
1 cup coconut milk or 1 packet coconut milk powder (maggi) mixed with 1½
cups of water, ½ tsp salt or to taste

1. Rub the fish well with besan, lemon juice, garlic paste, salt and pepper. Keep aside for 20 minutes. Drain, wash gently and pat dry with a kitchen towel.
2. Grind coconut, whole chillies, jeera, saboot dhania, haldi, imli, ginger, garlic and ½ cup water to a paste. Keep coconut paste aside.
3. Heat 4-5 tbsp oil in a kadhai. Add the onions & saute till golden brown.
4. Add the tomatoes and cook for 5-6 minutes or till oil separates.
5. Add the ground coconut paste, cook on slow fire for 8-10 minutes.
6. Add coconut milk. Boil, stirring in between. Add salt to taste. If the gravy appears to be thick add some more water and boil. Remove from fire.
7. Mix all the ingredients given under batter with ¼ cup water to get a thick batter. Dip the fish pieces in this batter and deep fry to a golden colour.
8. At the time of serving, add fish to the gravy and heat thoroughly. Serve.

Snacks

Special Paneer Pakore

Fragrant batter fried paneer cubes. Must give it a try.

Serves 3-4

200 gms paneer - cut into 8 big pieces

GRIND TOGETHER TO A PASTE
½" piece ginger, 2-3 flakes garlic
2 saboot kali mirch (peppercorns), 2 laung (cloves)
seeds of 2 chhoti illaichi (green cardamoms)
1 tsp jeera (cumin seeds), 2 tsp saboot dhania (coriander seeds)
¾" stick dalchini (cinnamon)
¾ tsp saunf (fennel)
½ tsp red chilli powder, ½ tsp salt

COATING
4 tbsp besan (gramflour)
2 tbsp thick curd
1 tbsp chopped fresh dhania
2 tsp kasoori methi (dry fenugreek leaves)

¼ tsp salt, ¼ tsp red chilli powder
¼ tsp ajwain (carom seeds)

1. Grind together ginger, garlic along with all the other ingredients to a fine paste. Use a little water if required.
2. Mix the ground paste with the paneer and cover with plastic wrap. Keep aside in the refrigerator till the time of serving.
3. At the time of serving, heat oil in a kadhai.
4. Sprinkle the coating ingredients on the paneer and mix well to coat. Add more besan if the paste does not stick to the paneer nicely.
5. Deep fry 2-3 pieces at a time till golden.
6. Serve hot with poodina chutney and serve with onion rings and lemon wedges.

Besani Murgi

Serves 3-4

400 gms chicken - cut into pieces or 6 legs (drumsticks)

¾ cup milk

1 tsp red chilli powder, ¾ tsp salt

GRIND TOGETHER TO A PASTE

½" piece ginger

2-3 flakes garlic

2 saboot kali mirch (peppercorns)

2 laung (cloves)

2 chhoti illaichi (green cardamoms)

1 tsp jeera (cumin seeds)

2 tsp saboot dhania (coriander seeds)

¾" stick dalchini

¾ tsp saunf (fennel)

COATING
8 tbsp besan, 6 tbsp curd
1 tbsp chopped fresh dhania
½ tsp salt, ¼ tsp red chilli powder
¼ tsp ajwain (carom seeds)

1. Grind together ginger, garlic along with all the saboot masalas. Use a little water if required. Keep the ground masala aside.
2. Mix together ¾ cup milk with ¼ cup water. Heat and bring to a boil.
3. Add the above ground masala, 1 tsp red chilli powder and ¾ tsp salt.
4. Add chicken also to the milk. Give 1-2 boils. Cover and lower heat. Cook for 8-10 minutes or till chicken is tender. Increase heat and cook till completely dry. Remove from fire. Cool.
5. To the cooked chicken add all the coating ingredients. Mix well.
6. Heat oil and fry 2-3 pieces at a time to a golden brown colour.
7. Serve hot with mint chutney, onion rings and lemon wedges

Note: Chops/Ribs can also be cooked in this manner. Only at stage 4, after 1-2 boils, give 2-3 whistles in a pressure cooker to ensure that the ribs get tender.

Dahi Bade

Makes 15

1½ cups (250 gm) urad dal - washed
½" piece ginger - very finely chopped
2 green chillies - chopped
½ tsp salt
¼ tsp soda-bicarb (mitha soda) or ½ tsp eno fruit salt
½ tsp jeera (cumin seeds), oil for frying

DAHI
3 cups curds - beat well till smooth
½ tsp powdered sugar
½ tsp red chilli powder, salt to taste
1 tsp bhuna jeera powder (roasted cumin, powdered)
¼ tsp kala namak (black salt)
15-20 kishmish (raisins) - soaked in water for 10 minutes
some chopped coriander to garnish

1. Wash and soak dal in enough water to cover the dal.
2. Soak it for 3 hours. Drain water and grind with the minimum amount of water to a paste. Do not over grind.
3. Add finely chopped ginger, green chillies and salt.
4. Add soda and beat well for 4-5 minutes till the mixture turns whitish and frothy. Add 2-3 tbsp hot water while beating.
5. Heat oil. With moistened hands, make badas with dal batter into 2" discs. Sprinkle some jeera seeds on it. Press lightly to stick the jeera and flatten the badas.
6. Deep fry 5-6 badas at a time in hot oil till they swell. Reduce heat to medium and turn the side. Fry on low medium heat till light golden. Drain from oil, keep aside.
7. Boil 6 cups water with 2 tsp salt. Remove from fire and add the badas. Soak in salted hot water for 5 minutes.
8. Press out water lightly and arrange badas in a flat dish.
9. Beat curd. Add all the ingredients to the curd. Pour curds on the arranged badas. Garnish with red chilli powder, chopped coriander and bhuna jeera powder. Serve with imli chutney & extra beaten curd.

Chicken Lollipops

A delicious snack made from chicken wings. The lollipops look like mini dumb bells. Remember to cover the end of the bone of the lollipops with a piece of foil.

Serves 3-4   *Picture on page 75*

600 gms lollipops

MIX TOGETHER

3 tsp ginger-garlic paste, 1 tsp salt
1½ tsp Kashmiri red chilli powder (degi mirch), 2 tsp amchoor powder
¾ tsp garam masala, a pinch of tandoori red colour, 4 tbsp maida

1. Mix all the ingredients together in a bowl. Add the lollipops in the mixture. Mix well. Let it marinate for 3-4 hours in the refrigerator.
2. At the time of serving, shape each piece to give them a neat look.
3. Shallow fry in a pan in 5-6 tbsp oil, turning sides or deep fry a few at a time till tender & crisp. If you shallow fry, keep the pan covered so that the chicken gets done while frying. Drain on a paper napkin. Serve.

Jalebi with Rabri: Recipe on page 100 ➢

Soya Balls

A nutritive & delicious snack, a hit both with adults as well as children. Do try it!

Makes 15

1 cup soya granules (nutri nugget granules)
100 gms paneer - grated (1 cup)
1 tsp garam masala
1 tsp salt
½ tsp red chilli powder
1½ tbsp tomato ketchup
2 tbsp green coriander - chopped
1 green chilli - finely chopped
oil for frying

FOR FRESH BREAD CRUMBS
2 bread slices - torn into pieces and churned in a mixer

1. Soak soya granules in 1 cup of hot water for 15 minutes.
2. Strain. Squeeze out the water well from the soya granules. (No water should remain).
3. For fresh bread crumbs, tear the bread slices into small pieces and churn at intervals in a mixer to get fine bread crumbs.
3. Mix paneer, fresh bread crumbs, garam masala, salt, red chilli powder, tomato ketchup, chopped green coriander, green chilli and the soya granules. Mix well.
4. Make small round balls out of the soya mixture.
5. Heat oil in a kadhai and deep fry the balls on medium heat till crisp and golden. Serve hot with tomato sauce.

Roti & Biryani

Lachha Parantha

Makes 6

2 cups atta (wheat flour), ½ tsp salt, 2 tbsp ghee, ½ cup milk, ½ cup water

1. Sift flour and salt in a paraat (deep bowl). Rub in 1 tbsp ghee till flour turns crumbly.
2. Mix water and milk together. Make a well in the middle of the flour. Pour milk-water mix gradually. Knead well to a dough of rolling consistency. Keep covered with a damp cloth for ½ hour.
3. Make 6 balls. Roll out each ball to a circle of 6" diameter. Spread some ghee all over. Sprinkle dry atta on half of the circle.
4. Fold into half to get a semi-circle. Spread ghee all over again. Put dry atta on half part of semi-circle. Fold again lengthwise into half so that you get a long strip.
5. Apply ghee all over on the strip. Roll the strip from one end till the end, to form a flattened ball (pedha). Press gently. Roll out, applying very

Contd...

little pressure, to form the lachha parantha. If too much pressure is applied, the layers stick to each other and do not open up later.

6. Stick in a heated tandoor or shallow fry on a tawa. Place on a clean napkin and crush the parantha slightly, to open up the layers. Serve hot.

Nan Badaami

Picture on page 1   *Makes 6*

2½ cups (250 gms) maida (plain flour)
½ cup hot milk
1 tsp baking powder
½ cup warm water (approx.)
½ tsp salt
6-8 badaam (almonds) - skinned & cut into long thin pieces (slivered)
1 tbsp kasoori methi

1. Heat milk and put it in a shallow bowl or a paraat. Add baking powder to the hot milk. Mix well and keep it aside for 1-2 minutes till it starts to bubble.

2. Sift maida and salt together. Add maida to the hot milk. Mix.
3. Knead to a dough with just enough warm water to get a dough of rolling consistency. Knead once again with wet hands till very smooth and elastic.
4. Keep covered with a damp cloth in a warm place for 3-4 hours.
5. Make 6-8 balls. Cover with a damp cloth and keep aside for 15 minutes.
6. Heat a gas tandoor for 10 minutes on fire.
7. Roll out each ball to an oblong shape. Spread ghee all over. Fold 1" from one side (lengthways), so as to overlap an inch of the nan. Press on the joint with the belan (rolling pin).
8. Sprinkle some blanched (skin removed by dipping in hot water) and chopped almonds and kasoori methi. Press with a rolling pin (belan) lightly. Pull one side of the nan to give it a pointed end like the shape of the nan.
9. Apply some water on the back side of the nan. Stick in a hot gas tandoor.
10. Cook till nan is ready. Spread butter on the ready nan and serve hot.

Khasta Keema Parantha

Serves 8

FILLING

250 gm keema (minced meat)
1 onion - chopped finely, 2 tsp ginger - chopped finely
1 tsp dhania powder, ½ tsp garam masala, 1 tsp salt, ½ tsp red chilli powder
2 green chillies - chopped, 1 tbsp finely chopped fresh coriander

DOUGH

2 cups atta (wheat flour), ½ tsp salt, 1 tbsp ghee

TOPPING

1 tbsp kasoori methi (dry fenugreek leaves)

1. To prepare the dough, sift flour and salt. Rub in 1 tbsp ghee. Add enough water to make a dough. Keep aside for 30 minutes.
2. For filling, heat 3 tbsp oil, add onion & fry till rich brown. Add keema (mince) and ginger and mix well. Reduce heat. Add salt, dhania powder, red chilli powder and garam masala. Fry for 1-2 minutes. Cook covered on low heat for about 5 minutes, till the mince is cooked.

3. Add green chillies and 1 tbsp finely chopped coriander. If there is any water, uncover and dry the mince on fire. Keep the stuffing aside.

4. For parantha, (see note) divide dough into 10 equal parts. Shape into round balls. Flatten each ball, roll out each into a round of 5" diameter. Spread 1 tsp full of ghee. Then spread 1-2 tbsp of filling all over.

5. Make a slit, starting from the centre till any one end. Start rolling from the slit, to form an even cone. Keeping the cone upright, press slightly.

6. Roll out, applying pressure only at the centre. Do not roll or press too much on the sides, otherwise the layers of parantha do not separate after cooking.

7. Sprinkle some kasoori methi and press with a rolling pin (belan).

8. Apply water on the back side of the parantha and stick carefully in a heated tandoor or place in a preheated oven in a greased tray.

9. Remove after a few minutes. Spread some ghee, serve hot.

Note: You can stuff the filling in an ordinary parantha and fry it on the tawa like any other bharwaan parantha. For bharwaan parantha roll out 2 small chappatis and sandwich them with keema filling. Press the sides well to seal the filling and roll out to a parantha.

Chicken Kali Mirch Pulao

*A delicious pulao with the colour and fragrance of pepper. Freshly ground pepper
gives a better flavour. Served with kachumber (minced salad) and yogurt, it
makes a complete meal.*

Serves 8

3 cups basmati rice
1 chicken (1 kg) - cut into pieces of your choice
2 cups peas (matar)
8 tbsp oil
5 tbsp pure ghee
1½ tsp jeera (cumin seeds)
12 saboot kali mirch (peppercorns)
3 moti illaichi (black cardamoms)
2" piece dalchini (cinnamon)
2 tej patta (bay leaves)
4 large onions - sliced
2 tsp ginger paste

2 tsp garlic paste
3½ tsp salt
3 tsp freshly ground pepper
2 tsp garam masala powder
4 tbsp finely chopped fresh dhania
4 tbsp lemon juice

1. Heat ghee and oil. Add jeera, kali mirch, moti illaichi, tej patta and dalchini. Fry till jeera turns brown.
2. Add sliced onions and fry till onion becomes dark brown.
3. Add ginger and garlic paste. Fry for 1-2 minutes.
4. Add chicken, peas, salt, pepper, garam masala and fresh dhania. Fry for 8-10 minutes. Cover on low heat for 5-6 minutes.
5. Add lemon juice and 6 cups of water.
6. When water boils add washed rice.
7. Mix well. Cover and lower heat. Cook for approximately 20 minutes or till rice is cooked and all the water has been absorbed.
8. Fluff rice with a fork and serve hot garnished with finely chopped tomatoes and fresh coriander.

Tandoori Platter with BBQ Sauce

Picture on cover   *Serves 8*

250 gm paneer - cut into large (1½") cubes, 2 capsicums - cut into large cubes
8 cherry tomatoes or 1 large tomato - cut into 8 pieces & pulp removed
200 gm (10-12) mushrooms - trim ends of the stalks, leaving them whole
100 gm baby corns - blanched with a pinch of haldi & 1 tsp salt in 3 cups water
1 onion - cut into fours & separated

MARINADE

1 cup thick curd - hang for 30 minutes, 2 tbsp thick cream, 2 tbsp oil
1 tbsp cornflour, 1 tbsp thick ginger-garlic paste
½ tsp black salt, ¼ tsp haldi or tandoori colour
2 tsp tandoori masala, ½ tsp red chilli powder, ¾ tsp salt or to taste

BARBECUE SAUCE

3 tbsp butter, 4-5 flakes garlic - crushed
2 large tomatoes - pureed till smooth, ¼ cup ready made tomato puree
¼ tsp red chilli powder, ½ tsp pepper, ¾ tsp salt or to taste, ¼ tsp sugar
½ tsp worcestershire sauce, ½ tsp soya sauce

RICE

1 cup uncooked rice - soaked for 1 hour
1 tbsp sugar, 2 tbsp oil
½ tsp jeera (cumin seeds)
2 small onions - sliced finely
1" stick dalchini (cinnamon)
2 tej patta (bay leaves), 2 laung (cloves)
2 chhoti illaichi (green cardamoms), 3-4 saboot kali mirch (peppercorns)
1 tsp salt or to taste

1. For rice mix sugar with 3 tbsp water in a small heavy bottomed vessel. Cook on low flame till it is rich brown in colour. Add two cups of hot water to it. Stir till dissolved. Remove from fire and keep aside.

2. Heat oil. Add jeera. When it turns golden add onions and stir fry till golden brown in colour.

3. Add the rice. Fry for a while. Add brown sugar water, all whole masalas and salt. Cover and cook on a very low fire till the water gets absorbed and the rice is done. Keep aside.

4. For vegetables, rub oil generously on a wire rack or grill of the oven.

Contd...

5. Mix all ingredients of the marinade. Add paneer, mushrooms and baby corns to the marinade and mix well to coat the marinade. Remove from bowl and arrange on the rack or on greased wooden skewers. In the remaining marinade which is sticking to the sides of the bowl, add onion, capsicum and tomatoes. Leave these in the bowl itself. Marinate all for atleast ½ hour.

6. Grill paneer & vegetables in the oven at 210°C/410°F for 12-15 minutes or roast in a gas tandoor, on the wire rack or on skewers. Spoon a little oil/melted butter (basting) on them. Add onion, capsicum and tomatoes. Grill for another 5-7 minutes.

7. For the sauce, heat oil in a kadhai. Add garlic & cook till light brown. Add tomatoes, tomato puree & chilli powder. Cook for 5 minutes till well blended. Add all other ingredients & ½ cup water to get a thin sauce. Boil. Simmer for 2 minutes. Remove from fire and keep aside.

8. To serve, heat rice seperately in a microwave or an oven. Spread the rice on a serving plate. Put some hot sauce on the rice. Arrange grilled vegetables on sauce with or without skewers. Pour some hot sauce over the vegetables. Serve the extra sauce in a separate sauce boat or bowl. Serve at once.

Sweets

Jalebi with Rabri

Picture on page 85   *Serves 8*

JALEBI

1 cup maida, 1 tbsp besan, ¼ tsp (level) soda bicarb
½ tbsp oil, ½ cup thick curd, ¾ cup warm water, oil or ghee for frying

SYRUP

1¼ cups sugar, ¾ cup water, 2-3 pinches orange-red colour

RABRI

4 cups full cream milk
75 gm khoya - grated, (½ cup)
2 tbsp sugar, 6-8 pistas - chopped
3 chhoti illaichi (green cardamoms) - powdered
rose petals or silver sheet (varq)

1. Boil milk in a heavy bottomed kadhai. Add khoya and sugar.
2. Simmer on low-medium heat for about 40-45 minutes, scraping the
   sides, till the quantity is reduced to almost half and the mixture turns

thick with a thick pouring consistency. Remove from fire. The rabri turns thick on keeping.

3. Add some chopped pistas and cardamom powdered into the mixture.
4. Transfer to a serving dish and garnish with pistas and rose petals.
5. Chill in the fridge till the time of serving time.
6. For jalebi, sieve maida, besan and soda. Add curd and oil. Add enough warm water (about ¾ cup) to make a batter of a soft dropping consistency.
7. Beat batter well till smooth. Cover and keep aside for 30-40 minutes.
8. Heat oil or ghee in a frying pan till medium hot. Put the batter in a piping bag and make circles within circle, starting from the outside.
9. Reduce heat. Fry them golden brown on low heat on both sides, turning carefully with a pair of tongs (chimta). Remove from oil, drain excess oil and keep aside.
10. For the syrup, boil sugar, water and colour in a kadhai. After the first boil keep on low flame for 5-7 minutes till a stringy syrup is attained.
11. At serving time, dip 4-5 jalebis at a time in the hot syrup for 1 minute, take out and serve them hot with rabri.

Phirni

Serves 6

3½ cups (700 gm) milk, ¼ cup basmati rice
¼ cup sugar plus 1 tbsp more, or to taste
4 almonds (badaam) - shredded, 5-6 green pistas (pistachio) - shredded
2 small silver leaves, optional, 2-3 chhoti illaichi (green cardamom) - powdered
1 drop kewra essence or 1 tsp ruh kewra, a few rose petals - to decorate

1. Soak rice of good quality for about an hour in a little water.
2. Drain rice & grind with 4-5 tbsp of water to a very fine & smooth paste. Mix the rice paste with ½ cup milk and make it thinner. Keep aside.
3. Mix the rice paste with all the milk in a clean, heavy bottomed pan. Cook on medium heat, stirring continuously and let it boil. Boil, stirring constantly for 2-3 minutes more to get a mixture of creamy consistency.
4. Add sugar and cardamom powder and mix well for a few seconds.
5. Remove from fire and add ruh kewra or the essence and half of the shredded almonds and pistachios.Pour the mixture into 6 small bowls.
7. Chill. Decorate each bowl with a silver leaf, a few nuts and rose petals.

Anjeeri Gobhi: Recipe on page 40, Achaari Bhindi: Recipe on page 49 ➢

$\mathscr{N}ita\ \mathscr{M}ehta's$ BEST SELLERS (Vegetarian)

All Time Favourite
SNACKS

SANDWICHES

Taste of RAJASTHAN

Desserts Puddings

ZERO OIL

Delicious Parlour
ICE-CREAMS

Indian Cooking
HANDI TAWA KADHAI

Different ways with
CHAAWAL

PASTA & CORN

PARTY FOOD

PANEER all the way

MENUS from around
the world